LAUGH OUT LOUD

Knock-Knocks, Jokes, and Tongue-Twisters

BARNES & NOBLE BOOKS

NEW YORK

Library of Congress Cataloging-in-Publication Data Available

10   9   8   7   6   5   4   3   2   1

Published by Sterling Publishing Co., Inc.
387 Park Avenue South, New York, NY 10016
©2005 by Sterling Publishing Co., Inc.

This book is comprised of materials from the Sterling titles:
Animal Jokes ©2003 by Sterling Publishing Co., Inc.
Silly Knock-Knocks ©2001 by Joseph Rosenbloom
Tricky Tongue Twisters ©2001 by Joseph Rosenbloom
Nutty Jokes ©2001 by Matt Rissinger and Phil Yates

Printed in China
All rights reserved

ISBN 0-7607-6783-1

Table of Contents

Tricky Tongue-Twisters

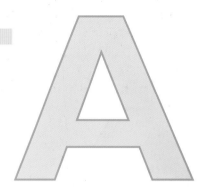

Aunt Edith's anteater.
Aunt Edith's anteater.
Aunt Edith's anteater.

Ava ate 80 eggs.
Ava ate 80 eggs.
Ava ate 80 eggs.

Ape cakes.
Ape cakes.
Ape cakes.

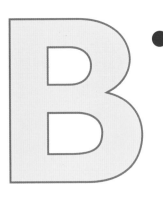

B

Build a big brick building.
Build a big brick building.
Build a big brick building

A box of biscuits.
A box of biscuits.
A box of biscuits.

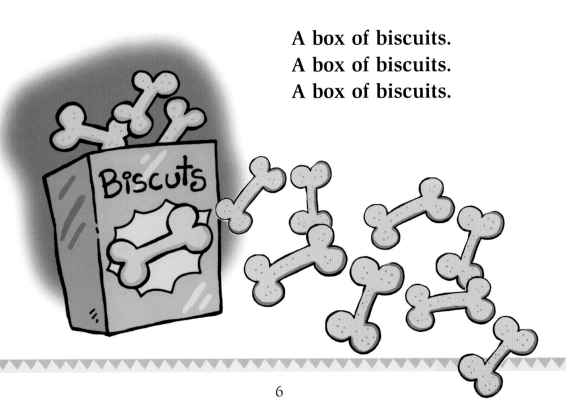

Rubber baby buggy bumpers.
Rubber baby buggy bumpers.
Rubber baby buggy bumpers.

How many times can you say this in ten seconds?
Brown, black, blue.

Bluebirds in blue birdbaths.
Bluebirds in blue birdbaths.
Bluebirds in blue birdbaths.

Bedbug's blood.
Bedbug's blood.
Bedbug's blood.

Betty Botter bought a bit of butter.
"But," said she, "this butter's bitter.
If I put in in my batter, it will make my batter bitter.
But a bit of better butter — that would make my
       batter better."
So Betty Botter bought a bit of better butter
(Better than her bitter butter)
And made her bitter butter
A bit better.

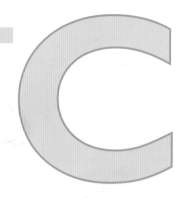

Crisp crust crackles.
Crisp crust crackles.
Crisp crust crackles.

Cheap sausage stew.
Cheap sausage stew.
Cheap sausage stew

Clean clams.
Clean clams.
Clean clams.

The fish and chip shop.
The fish and chip shop.
The fish and chip shop.

Tricky crickets.
Tricky crickets.
Tricky crickets.

Crisp cracker crumbs.
Crisp cracker crumbs.
Crisp cracker crumbs.

Chip's ship sank.
Chip's ship sank.
Chip's ship sank.

Carl called Claude.
Carl called Claude.
Carl called Claude.

Kooky cookies.
Kooky cookies.
Kooky cookies.

D

Don't you dare dawdle, Darryl!
Don't you dare dawdle, Darryl!
Don't you dare dawdle, Darryl!

A dozen dim ding-dongs.
A dozen dim ding-dongs.
A dozen dim ding-dongs.

Ducks don't dunk doughnuts.
Ducks don't dunk doughnuts.
Ducks don't dunk doughnuts.

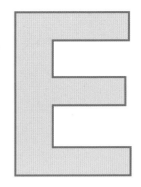

Eight eager eagles.
Eight eager eagles.
Eight eager eagles.

Edgar at 8 ate 8 eggs a day.
Edgar at 8 ate 8 eggs a day.
Edgar at 8 ate 8 eggs a day.

Elegant elephants.
Elegant elephants.
Elegant elephants.

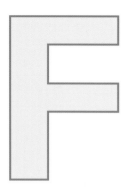

F

Fried fresh fish.
Fried fresh fish.
Fried fresh fish.

Fifteen filthy flying foxes.
Fifteen filthy flying foxes.
Fifteen filthy flying foxes.

Free kiwis.
Free kiwis.
Free kiwis.

Five fat French fleas.
Five fat French fleas.
Five fat French fleas.

Fresh figs.
Fresh figs.
Fresh figs.

Four flyers flip-flop.
Four flyers flip-flop.
Four flyers flip-flop.

*How many times can you say this
in ten seconds?*

Frisk Fisk first.

**Free fruit flies.
Free fruit flies.
Free fruit flies.**

**Freckle-faced Freddy fidgets.
Freckle-faced Freddy fidgets.
Freckle-faced Freddy fidgets.**

Frank flunked French.
Frank flunked French.
Frank flunked French.

Fleas fly from flies.
Fleas fly from flies.
Fleas fly from flies.

Frank's friend fainted.
Frank's friend fainted.
Frank's friend fainted.

G

Greek grapes.
Greek grapes.
Greek grapes.

Good blood, bad blood.
Good blood, bad blood.
Good blood, bad blood.

Goats and ghosts.
Goats and ghosts.
Goats and ghosts.

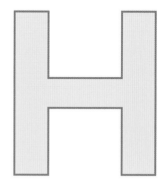

Hiccup teacup.
Hiccup teacup.
Hiccup teacup.

Has Hal's heel healed?
Has Hal's heel healed?
Has Hal's heel healed?

Hugh chooses huge shoes.
Hugh chooses huge shoes.
Hugh chooses huge shoes.

How many times can you say this in ten seconds?

Horse hairs are coarse hairs, of course.

Hurry, Harry!
Hurry, Harry!
Hurry, Harry!

A black spotted haddock.
A black spotted haddock.
A black spotted haddock.

I see Isa's icy eyes.
I see Isa's icy eyes.
I see Isa's icy eyes.

Ike ships ice chips.
Ike ships ice chips.
Ike ships ice chips.

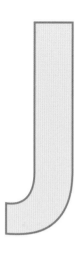

A gentle judge judges justly.
A gentle judge judges justly.
A gentle judge judges justly.

Jim jogs in the gym. Jane jogs in the jungle.

June sheep sleep soundly.

Come kick six sticks.
Come kick six sticks.
Come kick six sticks.

This disk sticks.
This disk sticks.
This disk sticks.

How many times can you say this in ten seconds?
Kirk's starched shirts.

Kooky kite kits.
Kooky kite kits.
Kooky kite kits.

L

Red leather. Yellow leather.
Red leather. Yellow leather.
Red leather. Yellow leather.

Little Ida lied a lot.
Little Ida lied a lot.
Little Ida lied a lot.

Lily Little lit a little lamp.
Lily Little lit a little lamp.
Lily Little lit a little lamp.

Luke likes licorice.
Luke likes licorice.
Luke likes licorice.

Lizzie's dizzy lizard.
Lizzie's dizzy lizard.
Lizzie's dizzy lizard.

*How many times can you say this
in ten seconds?*
Loose loops.

M

Mummies munch much mush.
Mummies munch much mush.
Mummies munch much mush.

Moses supposes his toeses are roses,
But Moses supposes erroneously.
For nobody's toeses are posies of roses
As Moses supposes his toeses to be.

How many times can you say this in ten seconds?
Michael's mouse munched muffins.

How many times can you say this in ten seconds?

No one knows Wayne.

**There's no need to light a night light
On a light night like tonight,
For a night light's just a slight light,
On a light night like tonight.**

**Norse myths.
Norse myths.
Norse myths.**

**Nineteen nice knights.
Nineteen nice knights.
Nineteen nice knights.**

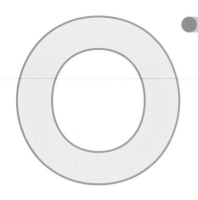

Old oily corks.
Old oily corks.
Old oily corks.

An oyster met an oyster,
And they were oysters two.
Two oysters met two oysters,
And they were oysters too.
Four oysters met a pint of milk,
And they were oyster stew.

Under the mother otter,
Uttered the other otter.

Plain bun, plum bun.
Plain bun, plum bun.
Plain bun, plum bun.

Peter Piper picked a peck of
  pickled peppers,
A peck of pickled peppers,
Peter Piper picked.
If Peter Piper picked a peck of
  pickled peppers,
Where's the peck of pickled
  peppers Peter Piper
  picked?

Peggy Babcock's mummy.
Peggy Babcock's mummy.
Peggy Babcock's mummy.

Painters, planters, pointers.
Painters, planters, pointers.
Painters, planters, pointers.

*How many times can you say this in
ten seconds?*

Penny penned a pretty poem.

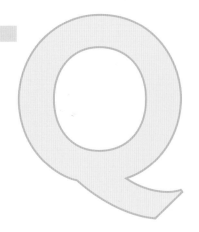

*How many times can you say this
in ten seconds?*

Quick kiss.

Quincy! Quack quietly or quit quacking!
Quincy! Quack quietly or quit quacking!
Quincy! Quack quietly or quit quacking!

R

Rigid wicker rockers.
Rigid wicker rockers.
Rigid wicker rockers.

*How many times can you say
this in ten seconds?*
   A well-read redhead.

The rhino wore a white ribbon.
The rhino wore a white ribbon.
The rhino wore a white ribbon.

Really rich roaches wear
wristwatches.

Raise Ruth's roof.
Raise Ruth's roof.
Raise Ruth's roof.

Red wrens' wings.
Red wrens' wings.
Red wrens' wings.

Robin robs wealthy widows.

S

Mrs. Smith's Fish Soup Shop.
Mrs. Smith's Fish Soup Shop.
Mrs. Smith's Fish Soup Shop.

The sun shines on shop signs.
The sun shines on shop signs.
The sun shines on shop signs.

Of all the smells I ever smelled,
I never smelled a smell
Like that smell I smelled smelt.

Six slick seals.
Six slick seals.
Six slick seals.

*How many times can you say
this in ten seconds?*
Spicy fish sauce.

**"Sure, the ship's
ship-shape, sir!"**

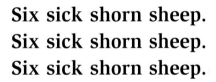

**Six sick shorn sheep.
Six sick shorn sheep.
Six sick shorn sheep.**

**Short swords.
Short swords.
Short swords.**

How many times can you say this in ten seconds?

Sloppy shortstops.

Sneak thieves seized the skis.
Sneak thieves seized the skis.
Sneak thieves seized the skis.

Stagecoach stops.
Stagecoach stops.
Stagecoach stops.

She sells seashells by the seashore.

Do thick tinkers think?
Do thick tinkers think?
Do thick tinkers think?

How many times can you say this
in ten seconds?
Thistle thorns stick.

A tutor who tooted a flute
Tried to tutor two tooters to toot.
Said the two to the tutor,
"Is it harder to toot
Or to tutor two tooters to toot?"

A tree toad loved a she-toad
That lived up in a tree.
She was a three-toed tree toad,
But a two-toed toad was he.

The two-toed toad tried to win
The she-toad's friendly nod,
For the two-toed toad loved the ground
On which the three-toed tree toad trod,

But no matter how the two-toed tree toad tried,
He could not please her whim.
In her three-toed bower, with her three-toed power,
The three-toed she-toad vetoed him.

Three free through trains.

Twelve trim twin-track tapes.
Twelve trim twin-track tapes.
Twelve trim twin-track tapes.

Tacky tractor trailer trucks.

Thick thistle sticks.

Ted sent Stan ten tents.
Ted sent Stan ten tents.
Ted sent Stan ten tents.

The U.S. twin-screw cruiser.
The U.S. twin-screw cruiser.
The U.S. twin-screw cruiser.

How many times can you say this in ten seconds?
Unique New York.

Uncle Upton's undies.
Uncle Upton's undies.
Uncle Upton's undies.

Vandals waxed Valerie's white van.
Vandals waxed Valerie's white van.
Vandals waxed Valerie's white van.

Valuable valley villas.
Valuable valley villas.
Valuable valley villas.

How many times can you say this in ten seconds?

Which veteran ventriloquist whistled?

Real wristwatch straps.

Whether the weather be fine
Or whether the weather be not;
Whether the weather be cold,
Or whether the weather be hot;
We'll weather the weather
Whatever the weather,
Whether we like it or not.

How many times can you say this in ten seconds?
    An itchy rich witch.

How much wood would a
    woodchuck chuck
If a woodchuck could
    chuck wood?
He would chuck the wood
    as much as he could
If a woodchuck could
    chuck wood.

White rings, round rings.
White rings, round rings.
White rings, round rings.

Wire-rimmed wheels.
Wire-rimmed wheels.
Wire-rimmed wheels.

X

Ex-disk jockey.
Ex-disk jockey.
Ex-disk jockey.

X-mas wrecks perplex and vex.
X-mas wrecks perplex and vex.
X-mas wrecks perplex and vex.

Yellow leather, red feather.

Yanking yellow yo-yos.
Yanking yellow yo-yos.
Yanking yellow yo-yos.

Local yokel jokes.

This is a zither.
Is this a zither?

What's big and white and lives in the Sahara Desert?
A lost polar bear.

What's a polar bear's favorite vacation spot?
Brrrr-muda.

What cartoon animal
weighs the least?
Skinny the Pooh.

What's brown and has 8 legs and a big trunk?
A spider coming home from a trip.

What kind of flowers would you give an absent-minded squirrel?
Forget-me-nuts.

What's an owl's favorite mystery?
A whooo-dunit.

What is a woodpecker's favorite kind of joke?
A knock-knock.

What would you call a lion that writes snappy songs?

King of the Jingle.

What would you get if you crossed a baby kangaroo with a TV buff?

A pouch potato.

What would you get if you crossed a guppy with a monkey?

A shrimpanzee.

Why don't fish go on-line?
Because they're afraid of being caught in the Net.

What kinds of doctors make fish look beautiful?
Plastic sturgeons.

What's an eel's favorite card game?
Glow Fish.

Where does a mother octopus shop for clothes for its children?
Squids 'R' Us.

What would you get if you crossed an octopus and a cat?
An animal with 8 arms and 9 lives.

Why did the turtle see a psychiatrist?
He wanted to come out of his shell.

What do cats use to keep their breath fresh?
Mouse wash.

What do baby cats wear?
Diapurrrrs.

How do you know when your cat's been on the Internet?
Your mouse has teeth marks in it.

What happened to the cat that swallowed a ball of wool?

It had mittens.

What do you call a cat with a pager?

A beeping tom.

What would you get if you crossed a cat with a porcupine?

An animal that goes "meowch" when it licks itself.

What did they name the dog
with the receding hairline?
Bald Spot.

What do you give a dog that
loves computers?
Doggie diskettes.

Why did the puppy go to the hair salon?
To get a shampoodle.

How do you turn a beagle into a bird?
Remove the B.

Why did the dog get a ticket?
For double barking.

What would you get if you crossed a dog with a chicken?
Pooched eggs.

What dinosaur always came in third in Olympic events?
Bronze-to-saurus.

What dinosaur was at home on the range?
Tyrannosaurus Tex.

In what age did the Sloppy-o-saurus live?
The Messy-zoic period.

Why are dinosaurs healthier than dragons?
Because dinosaurs don't smoke.

What do dragons like
most about school?
The fire drills.

Where do great dragons
end up?
In the Hall of Flame.

DRAGO the GREAT

What's big and gray and weighs down the front of your car?

An elephant in the glove compartment.

How do you know when there's an elephant in your chocolate pudding?

When it's lumpier than usual.

How can you tell the age of an elephant?

Count the candles on its birthday cake.

How do you give an
elephant a bath?
**First you find a
very large rubber
duckie.**

How many elephants does it take to program a computer?
**Four. One to work the keyboard and three to hold
down the mouse.**

What would you get if you crossed a parrot and
an elephant?
An animal that tells you everything it remembers.

What do snakes do after a fight?
They hiss and make up.

What is a snake's
favorite subject?
SSScience.

What kind of snake wears dark glasses and a
trench coat?
A spy-thon.

What would you get if you crossed a snake
with Bigfoot?
Ssss-quatch.

What would you call a
snake that drinks too
much coffee?
A hyper viper.

What would you get if you crossed an eight-foot snake
with a five-foot snake?
Nothing. Snakes don't have feet.

How do pigs store their computer files?
On sloppy disks.

Why did the computer squeak?
Because someone stepped on its mouse.

What do witches like to do on the computer?
Use the spell checker.

Why did the computer go to the eye doctor?
To improve its website.

What's a cat's favorite kind of computer?
A laptop.

What kind of computer mail do mice exchange?
Eeek-mail.

How do you make a cream puff?
Chase it around the block a few times.

What is a baker's favorite kind of book?
A who-donut.

What dessert can you eat in
the ocean?
Sponge cake.

Why did the banana go
to the hospital?
It didn't peel so good.

What did cavemen eat
for lunch?
Club sandwiches.

What's the pizza maker's motto?
Cheesy come, cheesy go.

Where do sheep buy their clothes?
Lamb shops.

Where do spies do their shopping?
At the snooper market.

What did the rip say to the pair of pants?
"Well, I'll be darned!"

Why does Superman wear such big shoes?
Because of his amazing feats.

What has four wheels and diaper rash?
A baby in a shopping cart.

What did the tie say to the hat?
"You go on ahead, I'll just hang around."

What do short-sighted ghosts wear?
Spook-tacles.

How do ghosts get to school?
On a ghoul bus.

What position did the
ghost play on the
soccer team?
Ghoulie.

Why didn't the skeleton go to the ball?
Because he had no body to go with.

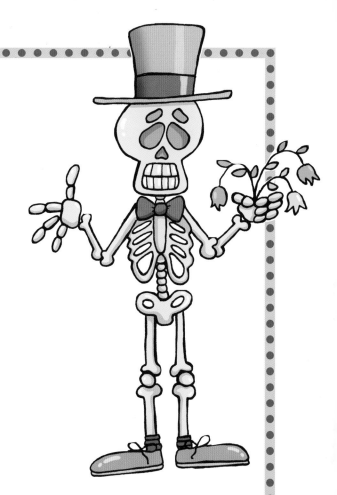

Why did the skeleton refuse to bungee jump?
He didn't have any guts.

What would you get if you crossed nursery rhymes with scary stories?
Mother Goosebumps.

What would you get if you crossed a vampire and a mummy?

Either a flying bandage or a gift-wrapped bat.

What do you call six vampires to go?

A Drac pack.

What would you get if you crossed a skunk with the Frankenstein monster?

Stinkenstein.

Why is it so hard to celebrate Father's Day in Egypt?
Because there are more mummies than daddies.

What was King Tut's favorite card game?
Gin Mummy.

What would you give King Kong for his birthday?
Anything he wants.

What was the butterfly's favorite subject?
Moth-ematics.

Why was the pony sent to the principal's office?
For horsing around.

Why was the chicken sent to the principal's office?
Because it kept pecking on the other kids.

What's dusty and gray and goes "Cough-cough!"

An elephant cleaning erasers.

What did the chalkboard say to the eraser?

"You rub me the wrong way."

What did the wad of gum say to the school desk?

"I'm stuck on you."

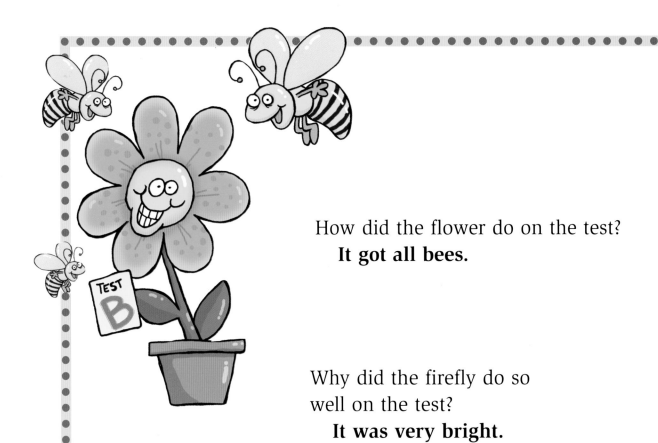

How did the flower do on the test?
It got all bees.

Why did the firefly do so
well on the test?
It was very bright.

What did the skeleton do before the big test?
It boned up.

Why did the cows get such low grades?
They copied off each udder.

Why did the squirrels get such low grades?
They drove the teacher nuts.

Why did the giant squids
get such low grades?
**They couldn't ink
straight.**

Why did King Kong wear a baseball glove to the airport?
He had to catch a plane.

Can kids learn to fly jet planes?
Yes, but they have to use training wheels.

What's gray, has 800 feet, and never leaves the ground?
An airplane full of elephants.

What kind of clothes do parachutists wear?
Jumpsuits.

Why don't dogs like to travel on planes?
They get jet wag.

What would you get if you crossed a blimp with an orangutan?
A hot-air baboon.

What swings through the trees and tastes good with milk?

Chocolate chimp cookies.

What has a nice trunk but never goes on a trip?

A tree.

Why did the tree go to the hospital?

For a sap-endectomy.

Why did the Christmas
tree go to the hospital?
It had tinsel-itis.

What do trees watch on
television?
Sap operas.

What grows on trees and is scared of wolves?
The three little figs.

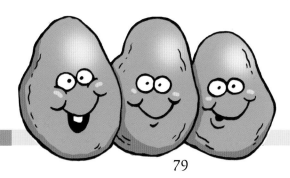

What do rabbits put on the backs of their cars?
Thumper stickers.

What kind of cars do rubber bands drive?
Stretch limos.

What did the little tire want to be when he grew up?
A big wheel.

What happens when a frog is double-parked on a lily pad?
It's toad away.

Why did the computer give up its car?
It was always crashing.

How come they never look for crooks in church?

Because crime doesn't pray.

What happened when the duck was arrested?

It quacked under pressure.

What did the security guard say to the firefly?

"Halt! Who glows there?"

What's yellow,
plastic, and holds
up banks?
A robber duckie.

Where do detectives sleep?
Under cover.

Why would Snow White make a great judge?
Because she is fairest of them all.

What would you get if you crossed a baseball player with a frog?

An outfielder who catches flies and then eats them.

Was the vampire race close?

Yes, it was neck and neck.

What kind of bee is always dropping the football?

A fumblebee.

At what sporting event can you find chicken and noodles?
The souper bowl.

What is a mummy's favorite sport?
Casketball.

What's a mouse's favorite sport?
Mice hockey.

What does a messy
flea need?
A lousekeeper.

What do videos do on their days off?
They unwind.

What would you get if you crossed a gardener
and a fortune teller?
Someone who weeds your palm.

What should you do if your smoke alarm goes off?
Run after it.

How do you keep your ears from ringing?
Get an unlisted head.

What should you do
if you find Godzilla in
your bed?
**Sleep in the guest
room.**

Knock-Knock.
  Who's there?
Afghanistan.
  Afghanistan who?
Afghanistan out here all day.

Knock-Knock.
  Who's there?
Althea.
  Althea who?
Althea later, Alligator!

Knock-Knock.
  Who's there?
Alaska.
  Alaska who?
Alaska my mother.

Knock-Knock.
Who's there?
Amen.
Amen who?
Amen hot water again.

Knock-Knock.
Who's there?
Anita.
Anita who?
Anita rest.

Knock-Knock.
Who's there?
Ammonia.
Ammonia who?
Ammonia a little kid.

Knock-Knock.
　Who's there?
Benny
　Benny who?
Benny long time no see.

Knock-Knock.
　Who's there?
Banana.

Knock-Knock.
　Who's there?
Banana.

Knock-Knock.
　Who's there?
Banana.

Knock-Knock.
　Who's there?
Orange.
　Orange who?
Orange you glad I didn't say Banana?

Knock-Knock.
  Who's there?
Barbie.
  Barbie who?
Barbie Q. Chicken.

Knock-Knock.
  Who's there?
Beth.
  Beth who?
Beth wishes, thweetie.

Knock-Knock.
  Who's there?
Barbara.
  Barbara who?
Barbara black sheep, have you any wool?

Knock-Knock.
Who's there?
Budapest.
Budapest who?
You're nothing Budapest.

Knock-Knock.
Who's there?
Butcher and Jimmy.
Butcher and Jimmy who?
Butcher arms around me and Jimmy a little kiss.

Knock-Knock.
Who's there?
Canoe.
Canoe who?
Canoe please get off my foot?

Knock-Knock.
Who's there?
Carmen.
Carmen who?
Carmen get it!

Knock-Knock.
Who's there?
Catch.
Catch who?
Bless you!

Knock-Knock.
　Who's there?
Cher.
　Cher who?
Cherlock Holmes.

Knock-Knock.
　Who's there?
Cain and Abel.
　Cain and Abel who?
Cain talk now, Abel tomorrow.

Knock-Knock.
　Who's there?
Celeste.
　Celeste who?
Celeste time I'm going to tell you!

Knock-Knock.
Who's there?
Datsun.
Datsun who?
Datsun old joke.

Knock-Knock.
Who's there?
Dexter.
Dexter who?
Dexter halls with boughs of holly...

Knock-Knock.
Who's there?
Doughnut.
Doughnut who?
Doughnut open until Christmas.

Knock-Knock.
Who's there?
Donahue.
Donahue who?
Donahue hide from me, you rat!

Knock-Knock.
Who's there?
Deluxe.
Deluxe who?
Deluxe Ness Monster.

Knock-Knock.
Who's there?
Dishes.
Dishes who?
Dishes the end of the road.

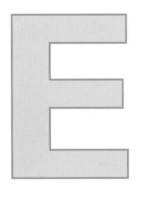

Knock-Knock.
Who's there?
Easter.
Easter who?
Easter anybody home?

Knock-Knock.
Who's there?
Eileen Dunn.
Eileen Dunn who?
Eileen Dunn the doorbell and it broke.

Knock-Knock.
Who's there?
Emerson.
Emerson who?
Emerson nice shoes you've got on.

Knock-Knock.
 Who's there?
Ezra.
 Ezra who?
Ezra no hope for me?

Knock-Knock.
 Who's there?
Emmet.
 Emmet who?
Emmet your service.

Knock-Knock.
 Who's there?
Evan.
 Evan who?
Evan to Betsy!

F

Knock-Knock.
Who's there?
Franz.
Franz who?
Franz forever!

Knock-Knock.
Who's there?
Fido.
Fido who?
Fido away, will you miss me?

Knock-Knock.
Who's there?
Fanny.
Fanny who?
**Fanny-body calls,
I'm out.**

Knock-Knock.
  Who's there?
Flea.
  Flea who?
Flea blind mice.

Knock-Knock.
  Who's there?
Freddie.
  Freddie who?
**Freddie or not, here
I come.**

Knock-Knock.
  Who's there?
Fletcher.
  Fletcher who?
Fletcher self go.

G

Knock-Knock.
  Who's there?
Gladys.
  Gladys who?
Gladys see you.

Knock-Knock.
  Who's there?
Goat.
  Goat who?
Goat to your room.

Knock-Knock.
  Who's there?
Gopher.
  Gopher who?
Gopher the gold!

Knock-Knock.
  Who's there?
Goliath.
  Goliath who?
Goliath down and go to sleep!

Knock-Knock.
  Who's there?
Greta.
  Greta who?
You Greta my nerves!

Knock-Knock.
  Who's there?
Gorilla.
  Gorilla who?
Gorilla cheese sandwich.

H

Knock-Knock.
Who's there?
Harvey.
Harvey who?
Harvey having fun yet?

Knock-Knock.
Who's there?
Howell.
Howell who?
**Howell you have your pizza,
plain or with sausage?**

Knock-Knock.
Who's there?
Hawaii.
Hawaii who?
I'm fine, how are you?

Knock-Knock.
　Who's there?
Hammond.
　Hammond who?
Hammond eggs.

Knock-Knock.
　Who's there?
Hugo.
　Hugo who?
Hugo your way and I'll go mine.

Knock-Knock.
　Who's there?
Hannah.
　Hannah who?
Hannah partridge in a pear tree.

Knock-Knock.
Who's there?
Iguana.
Iguana who?
Iguana hold your hand.

Knock-Knock.
Who's there?
Irish stew.
Irish stew who?
Irish stew would come out and play.

Knock-Knock.
Who's there?
Isabella.
Isabella who?
Isabella out of order?

Knock-Knock.
Who's there?
Izzy.
Izzy who?
Izzy come, Izzy go.

Knock-Knock.

Who's there?

Juno.

Juno who?

Juno what time it is?

Knock-Knock.

Who's there?

Justin.

Justin who?

Justin time for dinner.

Knock-Knock.

Who's there?

Jupiter.

Jupiter who?

Jupiter fly in my soup?

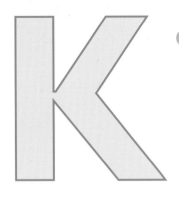

K

Knock-Knock.
  Who's there?
Kenny.
  Kenny who?
Kenny stay for dinner if he calls his mom?

Knock-Knock.
  Who's there?
Kareem.
  Kareem who?
Kareem of wheat.

Knock-Knock.
  Who's there?
Kimona.
  Kimona who?
Kimona my house.

Knock-Knock.
  Who's there?
Keith.
  Keith who?
Keith me, you fool.

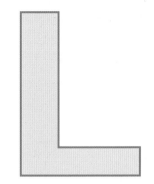

Knock-Knock.
   Who's there?
Little old lady.
   Little old lady who?
I didn't know you could yodel.

Knock-Knock.
   Who's there?
Lauren.
   Lauren who?
Lauren order.

Knock-Knock.
   Who's there?
Lion.
   Lion who?
Lion here on your doorstep till you open the door.

Knock-Knock.

Who's there?

Lettuce.

Lettuce who?

Lettuce in and we'll tell you another knock-knock joke.

Knock-Knock.

Who's there?

Luke.

Luke who?

Luke before you leap.

Knock-Knock.

Who's there?

Lois.

Lois who?

Lois man on the totem pole.

Knock-Knock.
  Who's there?
Megan, Elise, and Chicken.
  Megan, Elise, and Chicken who?
**Megan, Elise — and Chicken it
twice, gonna find out who's
naughty and nice...**

Knock-Knock.
  Who's there?
Mandy.
  Mandy who?
Mandy lifeboats — the ship's sinking!

Knock-Knock.
  Who's there?
Marmalade.
  Marmalade who?
**"Marmalade an egg,"
said the little chicken.**

Knock-Knock.
Who's there?
Nona.
Nona who?
Nona your business.

Knock-Knock.
Who's there?
Needle.
Needle who?
Needle little lunch.

Knock-Knock.
Who's there?
Nana.
Nana who?
Nana your business.

Knock-Knock.
   Who's there?
Nettie.
   Nettie who?
Nettie as a fruit-cake.

Knock-Knock.
   Who's there?
Nadya.
   Nadya who?
Nadya head if you understand what I'm saying.

Knock-Knock.
   Who's there?
N. E.
   N. E. who?
N. E. body home?

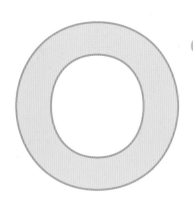

Knock-Knock.
Who's there?
Oink oink.
Oink oink who?
Are you a pig or an owl?

Knock-Knock.
Who's there?
Olivia.
Olivia who?
Olivia me alone!

Knock-Knock.
Who's there?
Omar.
Omar who?
Omar goodness gracious — wrong door!

Knock-Knock.
Who's there?
Oscar and Greta.
Oscar and Greta who?
Oscar foolish question, and Greta a foolish answer.

Knock-Knock.
Who's there?
Ohio.
Ohio who?
Ohio Silver!

Knock-Knock.
Who's there?
Omega.
Omega who?
Omega up your mind.

P

Knock-Knock.
   Who's there?
Police.
   Police who?
Police open the door.

Knock-Knock.
   Who's there?
Philippa.
   Philippa who?
Philippa bathtub, I'm dirty.

Knock-Knock.
   Who's there?
Pasta.
   Pasta who?
Pasta pizza.

Knock-Knock.
   Who's there?
Queen.
   Queen who?
Queen up your room.

Knock-Knock.
   Who's there?
Quacker.
   Quacker who?
Quacker nother bad joke and I'm leaving.

Knock-Knock.
   Who's there?
Quebec.
   Quebec.
Quebec to the end of the line.

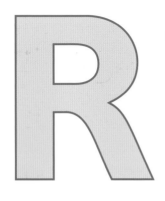

Knock-Knock.
   Who's there?
Rocky.
   Rocky who?
Rocky-bye baby, on the treetop...

Knock-Knock.
   Who's there?
Rhoda.
   Rhoda who?
Rhoda boat.

Knock-Knock.
   Who's there?
Ringo.
   Ringo who?
Ringo round the collar.

Knock-Knock.
   Who's there?
Raven.
   Raven who?
Raven maniac.

Knock-Knock.
   Who's there?
Sancho.
   Sancho who?
Sancho a letter but you never answered.

Knock-Knock.
   Who's there?
Siam.
   Siam who?
Siam your old pal.

Knock-Knock.
   Who's there?
Schick.
   Schick who?
Schick as a dog.

Knock-Knock.
   Who's there?
Sarah.
   Sarah who?
Sarah doctor in the house?

Knock-Knock.
   Who's there?
Siamese.
   Siamese who?
Siamese-y to please.

Knock-Knock.
   Who's there?
Senior.
   Senior who?
Senior through the keyhole, so I know you're in there.

Knock-Knock.
　Who's there?
Theresa.
　Theresa who?
Theresa fly in my soup.

Knock-Knock.
　Who's there?
Toothache.
　Toothache who?
Toothache the high road and I'll take the low road....

Knock-Knock.
　Who's there?
Trigger.
　Trigger who?
Trigger treat!

Knock-Knock.
 Who's there?
Unaware.
 Unaware who?
Unaware is what you put on first in the morning.

Knock-Knock.
 Who's there?
Uganda.
 Uganda who?
Uganda lot of weight.

Knock-Knock.
 Who's there?
Unity.
 Unity who?
Unity sweater for me?

Knock-Knock.
  Who's there?
Venice.
  Venice who?
Venice lunch?

Knock-Knock.
  Who's there?
Vanessa.
  Vanessa who?
Vanessa you going to grow up?

Knock-Knock.
  Who's there?
Vilma.
  Vilma who?
**Vilma frog turn into
a prince?**

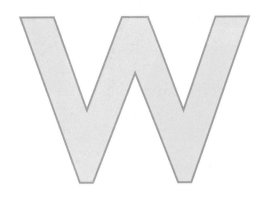

Knock-Knock.
   Who's there?
Weasel.
   Weasel who?
Weasel while you work...

Knock-Knock.
   Who's there?
Weirdo.
   Weirdo who?
Weirdo you think you're going?

Knock-Knock.
   Who's there?
Wendy Katz.
   Wendy Katz who?
**Wendy Katz away,
the mice will play.**

Knock-Knock.
  Who's there?
Willoughby.
  Willoughby who?
Willoughby my valentine?

Knock-Knock.
  Who's there?
Willie.
  Willie who?
Willie or won't he?

Knock-Knock.
  Who's there?
Will you remember me in a week?
  Yes.
Will you remember me in a month?
  Yes.
Will you remember me in a year?
  Yes.
Will you remember me in five years?
  Yes.
Knock-Knock.
  Who's there?
See? You've forgotten me already!

Knock-Knock.
  Who's there?
Xavier breath.
  Xavier breath who?
Xavier breath — I'm not listening.

Knock-Knock.
  Who's there?
X.
  X who?
X for breakfast.

Knock-Knock.
  Who's there?
X.
  X who?
X me no questions, I'll tell you no lies.

Knock-Knock.
  Who's there?
Yah.
  Yah who?
Ride 'em, cowboy!

Y

Knock-Knock.
  Who's there?
Yachts.
  Yachts who?
Yachts new?

Knock-Knock.
  Who's there?
Yule.
  Yule who?
Yule be sorry!

Knock-Knock.
  Who's there?
Yeti.
  Yeti who?
Yeti nother knock-knock joke.

Knock-Knock.
  Who's there?
Yuma.
  Yuma who?
Yuma best friend.

Knock-Knock.
  Who's there?
Yule.
  Yule who?
Yule never guess.

Knock-Knock.
  Who's there?
Zipper.
  Zipper who?
Zipper dee-doo-dah!

Knock-Knock.
  Who's there?
Zizi.
  Zizi who?
Zizi when you know how.

Knock-Knock.
  Who's there?
Zoe.
  Zoe who?
Zoe have come to the end of the chapter!

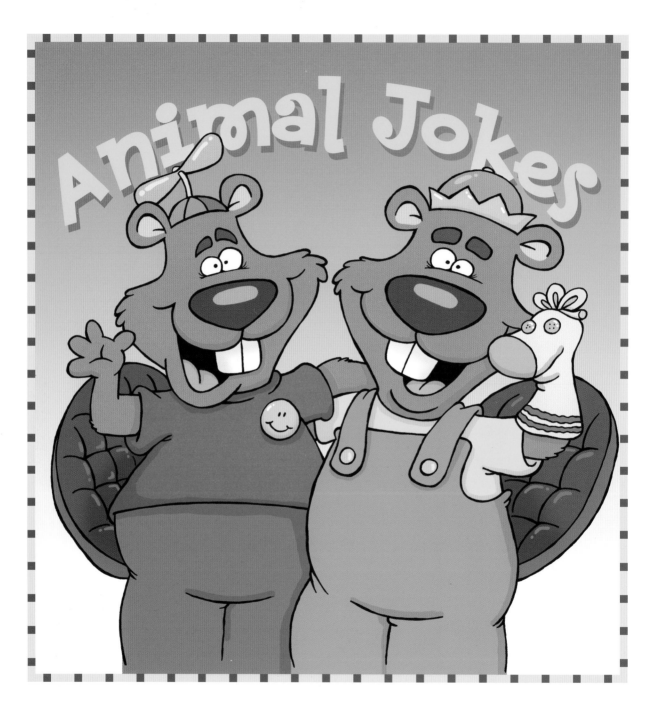

How many animals did Moses take on the ark?
Moses didn't take anything on the ark.
Noah did!

What animals were the last to leave the ark?
Elephants. They had to pack their trunks.

What animals didn't come on the ark in pairs?
Worms. They came in apples.

Knock-Knock.
Who's there?
Noah.
Noah who?
Noah good knock-knock joke?

What's black and white and green?
A seasick zebra.

What's black and white and blue all over?
A skunk at the North Pole.

What is black and white and lives in Hawaii?
A lost penguin.

What has to crawl 12 times to go a foot?
An inchworm.

Why did the worm oversleep?
Because it didn't want to get caught by the early bird.

What's the best way to get rid of a 100-pound worm in your garden?
Get a 1,000-pound robin.

What insect breathes fire?
A dragonfly.

What insect can't say
yes or no?
A may-bee.

How do fleas travel?
They itchhike.

What's green and goes, "Clomp, clomp,
clomp, clomp, clomp, clomp"?
**A grasshopper trying out his new
hiking boots.**

What would you get if you crossed a praying
mantis and a termite?
**An insect that says grace before eating your
house.**

Where do bugs buy their groceries?
At the flea market.

What has fifty legs but can't walk?
Half a centipede.

What would you get if you crossed a
centipede and a parrot?
A walkie-talkie.

Why don't centipedes
play football?
**By the time they
get their shoes on,
the game is over.**

What do bees say to each other when they come home?
"Hi, honey!"

What did the bee say to the flower?
"Hey, bud, what time do you open?"

How do stinging insects talk to each other on a computer?
They use bee-mail.

How did the bee get to school?
It took a buzz.

Why did the bee go to the doctor?

It had hives.

What is a bee with a low buzz?

A mumble bee.

What is a bee's favorite country?

Stingapore.

Knock-Knock.

Who's there?

Honeybee.

Honeybee who?

Honeybee nice and open the door.

Knock-Knock.
　Who's there?
Owl goes.
　Owl goes who?
Yes, I know it does.

What do birds eat for dessert?
　Chocolate chirp cookies.

Why do birds fly south for
the winter?
　**They don't want to wait
　for the bus.**

Who do birds marry?
　Their tweethearts.

What birds hang out around the ski slopes?
Skigulls.

What do you call a bird in winter?
A brrrd.

Why was the little bird punished at school?
It was caught peeping during a test.

What bird is always around when there's something to eat or drink?
The swallow.

What size T-shirt should you buy for a 200-pound egg?
Eggs-tra large.

Why didn't the omelet laugh?
>**It didn't get the yolk.**

What would you get if you crossed an earthquake and a chicken?
>**Scrambled eggs.**

What would you get if you crossed a chicken and a guitar?
>**A chicken that plucks itself.**

Why did the chicken cross the road twice?
Because she was a double-crosser.

What did the chicken say when she
laid a square egg?
"Ouch!"

Why did the hen go
to the doctor?
To get a chick-up.

Why was the chicken
sick?
It had people pox.

What bird hunt is
never successful?
A wild goose chase.

Why do people get
goose bumps?
**Because camel bumps
are too big.**

Why did the goose cross the road?
To get a gander at the other side.

What would you get if you crossed a goose and a
rhinoceros?
An animal that honks before it runs you over.

Who stole the soap?
The robber ducky.

What is a duck's favorite snack?
Quacker jacks.

If a duck says, "Quack, quack," when it walks, what does it say when it runs?
"Quick, quick!"

What did the lady duck say to the sales clerk when she bought a lipstick?
"Please put it on my bill."

What two dogs are opposites?
Hot dogs and chili dogs.

How does a hot dog wear its hair?
In a bun.

What do you call the top of a dog house?
The woof.

Does your dog bite strangers?
Only when he doesn't know them.

How do you cure fleas on a dog?
It all depends on what's wrong with the fleas.

Why do dogs make better pets than elephants?
Elephants keep getting stuck in the front door.

Why do fire trucks
have dogs on them?
**To find the fire
hydrant.**

Is your dog paper-
trained?
**No, he can't read
a thing.**

If dogs go to obedience school, where do cats go?
Kittygarten.

What magazine do cats like to read?
Good Mousekeeping.

Knock-Knock.
Who's there?
Lettie.
Lettie who?
Lettie cat out of the bag.

What cat likes to go bowling?
An alley cat.

If there were ten cats in a boat and one jumped out, how many would be left?

None, because they were all copycats.

Where do cats go to dance?

To the fur ball.

What cat lives in the ocean?

An octopus.

Why wouldn't they let the cat use the computer?

She kept chasing the mouse.

When does a mouse weigh as much as an elephant?
When the scale is broken.

What's the difference between mice and rice?
You can't throw mice at weddings.

When is it bad luck to have a black cat follow you?
When you're a mouse.

Knock-Knock.
Who's there?
Flea.
Flea who?
Flea blind mice.

Where do frogs sit?
On toadstools.

What is a frog's favorite flower?
A crocus.

How did the frog win
the jumping race?
**By leaps and
bounds.**

What is a frog's
favorite soft drink?
Croak-a-cola.

Why does a turtle live in a shell?
Because it can't afford an apartment.

Why is it great to be a turtle?
You never have far to walk home.

Where does a turtle go out to eat?
In a slow-food restaurant.

What do you say to speed up a turtle?
"Make it snappy."

What do you call a rabbit that is owned by a beetle?
A bug's bunny.

What is the opposite of the Easter bunny?
The Wester bunny.

Where do rabbits go
to hear people sing?
To the hopera.

Where do you find
flying rabbits?
In the hare force.

What would you get if you crossed a robot and a skunk?

R 2 PU.

What is the most famous skunk statue in Egypt?

The Stinx.

If a skunk wrote a popular book, what list would it be on?

The best smeller list.

What would you get if you crossed a skunk with a fairy?

Stinkerbell.

How did the sick sheep get to the hospital?
By lambulance.

Dogs have fleas. What do sheep have?
Fleece.

Knock-Knock.
Who's there?
Babar.
Babar who?
Babar black sheep.

Why didn't the lamb make a sound all day?
It didn't like to bleat between meals.

What gives milk and has two wheels?
A cow on a motorcycle.

What would you get if you crossed a kangaroo
with a cow?
A kangamoo.

Why did the cow cross
the road?
**To get to the udder
side.**

What do cows read in
the morning?
The moos-paper.

What cheese does a cow like?
Moo-zarella.

What did the mama cow say to the baby cow?
It's pasture bedtime.

Knock-Knock.
   Who's there?
Cows.
   Cows who?
No — cows moo.

What do cows say
when they cry?
"Moo-hoo!"

Why didn't the horse draw
the cart?
He couldn't hold a pencil.

What did the horse say after
it finished its hay?
"That was the last straw."

Why did the horse put on the blanket?
He was a little colt.

Why aren't horses well dressed?
They wear shoes but no socks.

What kind of vehicle does a hog drive?
A pig-up truck.

What number does a pig call in an emergency?
Swine-one-one.

What's a pig's favorite
fairy tale?
Slopping beauty.

What position does a pig
play in baseball?
Short slop.

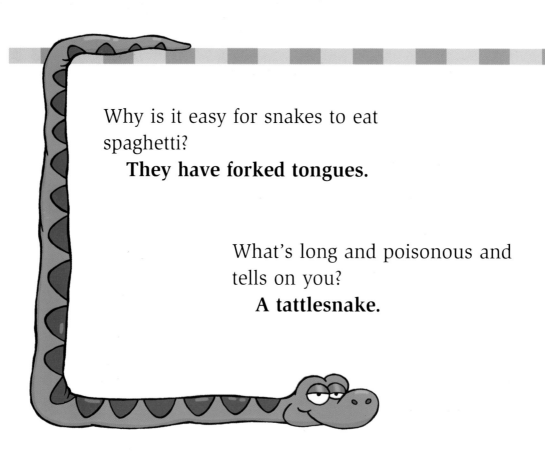

Why is it easy for snakes to eat spaghetti?
They have forked tongues.

What's long and poisonous and tells on you?
A tattlesnake.

How do snakes sign their letters?
Love and hisses.

Why do they measure snakes in inches?
Because they have no feet.

What is long and thin and goes "Hith, Hith"?
A snake with a lisp.

Why did the baby
snake cry?
It lost its rattle.

Why is it so hard to play
a joke on a snake?
You can't pull its leg.

Knock-Knock.
Who's there?
Snake.
Snake who?
**"Snake me out to the
ball game..."**

What's the difference between a dog and a marine scientist?

One wags a tail, the other tags a whale.

Who watches little squids?

Babysquidders.

What sea creature can add?

An octo-plus.

What is the hardest thing about being an octopus?
Washing your hands before dinner.

What goes, "Clomp, clomp, clomp, clomp, clomp, clomp, clomp, squish"?
An octopus with one shoe off.

What do whales chew?
Blubber gum.

What do clams and oysters do over the holidays?
Shellebrate.

Who grants the wishes of fishes?
Their fairy codmother.

What's the difference between a fish and a piano?
You can't tune a fish.

What do you call a fish without an eye?
A fsh.

Why don't fish play tennis?
They don't want to get caught in the net.

Why did the otter cross the road?
To get to the otter side.

Where do otters come from?
Otter space.

Knock-Knock.
Who's there?
Otter.
Otter who?
**Otter apologize for
some of these jokes.**

What snack do little monkeys have with their milk?
Chocolate chimp cookies.

What monkey can fly?
A hot air baboon.

What language do chimpanzees speak?
Chimpanese.

What did the monkey say to the vine?
"Thanks for letting me hang around."

What did the leopard say in the cafeteria?
"Save me a spot."

How do bears like campers?
Raw.

Why do leopards have spotted coats?
Because the tigers bought all the striped ones.

What would you get if you crossed a tiger with a Japanese restaurant?
Man-eating sushi.

Knock-Knock.
Who's there?
Lionel.
Lionel who?
Lionel roar if you don't feed it.

What weighs 2,000 pounds and is covered with lettuce and special sauce?

A big MacElephant.

Why do elephants have wrinkled ankles?

They tie their sneakers too tight.

Why don't elephants tip bellhops?

They like to carry their own trunks.

Why do elephants have trunks?

Because they can't fit all their stuff in their makeup case.

Why are elephant rides cheaper than pony rides?

Because elephants work for peanuts.

What elephant flies?

A Dumbo jet.

How can you tell that an elephant is living in your house?

By the enormous pajamas in your closet.

How can you tell if an elephant is in your cereal box?

Read the label.

Why do bears have fur?
**So their underwear
won't show.**

What bear loves to wash
her hair?
Winnie the Shampoo.

What's a polar bear's favorite cereal?
Ice Krispies.

Why does a mink have fur?
If it didn't, it would be a little bear.

What would you get if you crossed a greyhound with a giraffe?

A dog that chases airplanes.

Can giraffes have babies?

No, they can only have giraffes.

What is worse than a giraffe with a sore throat?

An octopus with tennis elbow.

Does a giraffe get a sore throat if it gets wet feet?

Yes, but not until the following week.

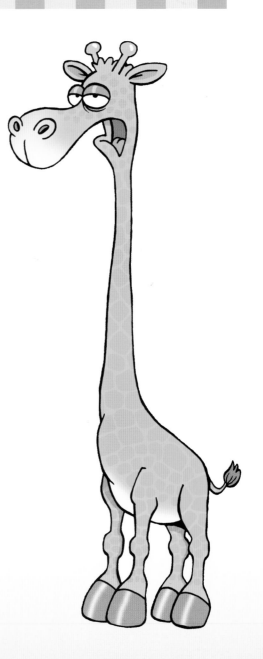

What would you get if you crossed a kangaroo and a crocodile?
Leaping lizards.

What newspaper do reptiles read?
The Scaly News.

What is a sick crocodile?
An illigator.

What does an alligator sing?
Scales.

What is it called when two spiders get married?
A webbing.

On what day do spiders have a good meal?
Flyday.

What do spiders eat with their hamburgers?
French flies.

SPIDER: Will you share your curds with me?
MISS MUFFET: No whey.

How does one amoeba speak to another amoeba?
On a cell phone.

What do you call a whale that talks too much?
A blubbermouth.

What would you get if you crossed a parrot and a caterpillar?
A chatterpillar.

Knock-Knock.
Who's there?
Hyena.
Hyena who?
Hyena tree sat a parrot.

What jungle animal is always complaining?
A whinoceros.

Index